CW00602059

Curator's welcome

Thank you for taking the time to visit Dawyck Botanic Garden today. I have been very lucky to have worked here for 25 years and in that time have gained a great deal of satisfaction working with this wonderful and unique plant collection. With so much to see in any season, Dawyck is truly an all-year-round Garden, renowned as home to one of Scotland's finest tree collections.

A garden offers many things to many people, a place of quiet contemplation, somewhere for exercise and stimulation, or a place with amazing plants to discover. Our series of self-guided trails allow you to explore the Garden, and our collection, at your own pace, and to suit your own interests. Follow the Native Tree Trail for a chance to marvel at Scottish trees, or the Majestic Tree Trail to view treasures from China, Japan, Nepal, Chile and around Europe. At Dawyck it really is possible to go round the world in an afternoon!

We pride ourselves on the quality of our visitors' experience. From the five-star welcome to the quality of the home-cooked fayre in the café, a visit won't disappoint. And, as our gold award in Green Tourism shows, we match the importance of our visitor experience with our environmental principles. You can view our modern re-created early Victorian hydro-electric system, which provides power to the garden buildings and exports any surplus to the National Grid. This technology, along with many other green initiatives, has secured Dawyck's place as a leader in reducing our carbon footprint. A visit to Dawyck is an opportunity to see at first-hand how we care about our impact on the environment.

Dawyck has lots to offer for everyone, I hope you enjoy your visit and return soon.

Graham Stewart
Curator, Dawyck Botanic Garden

Contents

Introduction	1
The history of the Garden	2
What to see at the Garden	5
Scrape Glen	9
Chapel Bank	11
A green Garden	13
Endangered conifers	15
Dawyck's natural history	17
Dawyck through the seasons –	
Spring and summer	19
Autumn and winter	21
Managing the collection	23

Introduction

Located on the upper reaches of the mighty River Tweed, Dawyck Botanic Garden spans 26ha (65 acres) of beautiful Borders hillside, ranging from 165 to 250 metres above sea-level. Due to its position inland and this elevation, the Garden enjoys an almost continental climate: warm dry summers, with temperatures up to 25°C, and cold winters which can drop down to -20°C, with snow covering the ground for weeks at a time. Plants from cooler montane regions of the world thrive here, and the unique collection of trees makes this Garden one of the finest arboreta in the world.

Dawyck is an 18th-century designed landscape, hundreds of years of horticultural, arboricultural and silvicultural tradition with a very modern purpose and outlook. Many of the specimens planted here were the first examples brought to Scotland and our staff continue collecting plants to grow at Dawyck, although for different reasons. By the time the Garden passed into the care of the Royal Botanic Garden Edinburgh (RBGE), several of the tree specimens planted by previous owners of the land had become endangered in their natural habitats. This set the tone for what has become a sanctuary for endangered plants, a collection not only for conservation and study, but, as originally intended, a place of beauty to be enjoyed.

The Royal Botanic Garden Edinburgh – four Gardens, one Collection

Dawyck is one of the Regional Gardens of RBGE, four Gardens in Scotland that comprise one of the world's richest collections of plants, containing over 13,500 species from 156 countries and including some that are extinct in the wild and others that are new to science. With the lowest temperatures of our four Garden sites, Dawyck is the perfect habitat to grow plants from mountainous regions of Europe, China, Nepal, Japan and North America. The plantings in the Garden are grouped geographically so you can get a feel for the variation in these habitats.

Botanic gardens play a vital role in modern-day conservation and RBGE is actively involved in science and conservation in many countries around the world. Of the plant species grown at Dawyck, 186 are under threat in their native habitat, with one now extinct in the wild and 43 more critically endangered. The Garden is one of many key botanic 'safe sites' that are actively involved in the preservation of the world's plants.

The history of the Garden

The history of the Garden still informs its structure today, with each different owner of this land making an impact on the landscape. When RBGE took over the arboretum of the Dawyck estate in 1979, we inherited an incredible tradition of plant collection and stewardship, resulting in an extraordinary and diverse landscape. The Veitch family, owners of the estate from 1491 to 1691, planted the first horse chestnuts (*Aesculus hippocastanum*) and silver firs (*Abies alba*) in Scotland at Dawyck. One of the latter can still be seen at the Garden well over 300 years later, and is amongst the oldest trees in RBGE's Living Collection.

F.R.S. Balfour pictured with some of the many Rhododendrons he brought to Dawyck

Fagus sylvatica in autumn

Acer palmatum in autumn

In 1691, John Veitch sold the estate to Sir James Naesmyth and this new laird undertook a fresh phase of planting at the garden. Introductions at this time included European larch (*Larix decidua*) which can still be seen in the Garden. Sir James' grandson, Sir John Naesmyth, discovered the famous upright beech (*Fagus sylvatica* 'Dawyck') and also planted 809 ha (2,000 acres) of mixed woodlands at the estate. He further shaped the landscape by investing in several plant-hunting expeditions to Asia and North America, which resulted in exciting new collections.

When, in 1897, the Dawyck Estate was sold into the Balfour family, F.R.S, or Fred, Balfour undertook the planting of hundreds of rhododendrons and many thousands of daffodils. He collected plants in North America, and continued in the path

of Sir John Naesmyth, investing in expeditions and building contacts that led to important new specimens for the Garden from plant hunters such as Ernest 'Chinese' Wilson, George Forrest, Reginald Farrer and Frank Kingdon Ward. Balfour's son took over the estate in 1945 and tended it until 1968 when a hurricane took down 50,000 trees from the hillside and changed the face of the Garden forever. In 1978, the family gave the woodland garden of the estate to the nation and RBGE took over the stewardship the following year.

The shift to becoming a botanic garden has changed this landscape again. A growing focus on conservation and habitat loss, and the challenge of preserving plant biodiversity, altered the way the Garden was used. Allowing the collection to be accessible for research and as an educational resource, as well as open to visitors, meant increasing the number of paths and bridges and clearing the landscape. The Visitor Centre provides a home for our active programme of events, guided tours, talks, courses and classes, while the studio hosts local arts and crafts exhibitions, making Dawyck a hub for the community and for learning. New plant collecting expeditions have bolstered the wild-origin plantings at the Garden, taking the history back full circle to the times of the Veitches and Naesmyths, whose own plantings often now represent species endangered in their own habitats. Our focus on responsible environmental management, and the impact of the Garden itself on the landscape, means that the unique environment of this special Garden can continue long into the future.

What to see at the Garden

Azalea Terrace – Bisecting the Garden east to west, in the late spring to early summer this area is a wonder of colour and scent. Many hardy hybrid azaleas give rise to one of the most popular picture postcard views of the Garden.

Beech Walk – One of the many marvels of Dawyck, this is a grand stepped terrace cut out of the hillside, which gives a regal walk alongside an avenue of young copper beech. This is the second generation avenue, established to replace the original which succumbed to over-maturity. The Walk has views beyond the Garden to the rolling Meldon Hills and an eagle-eye-view over Dawyck House.

The Azalea Terrace in full flower

The Heron Wood Reserve – Established as a cryptogamic sanctuary in 1993, this untended area of the Garden allows the growth and development of fungi (including lichens), bryophytes (mosses, liverworts and hornworts), pteridophytes (ferns and horsetails) and algae. This group makes up around 84% of the world's botanical diversity. RBGE is a world leader in cryptogam research and this 3.5 ha (7.5 acre) area is now one of the best documented pieces of land in Britain.

Dynamo Pond – Originally established as a man-made pond by damming the Scrape Burn, the pond served as the header tank for an early Victorian hydro-electric scheme. It now supplies water once again for our modern hydro turbine system and serves as the catchment for the Garden's water supply.

Lichen species growing in Heron Wood

Puffball fungi

Salix lanata

Scottish Plants – Botanic gardens are often associated with conservation efforts and collections from overseas, so it is easy to forget that threatened habitats also exist at home. Look for the woolly willow (*Salix lanata*), a plant threatened in its native habitat by overgrazing, which RBGE has successfully reintroduced to the wild.

Shaw Brae – The Shaw Brae area is a conifer-lover's paradise with many early introductions of unusual conifers, including the Brewer's weeping spruce (*Picea breweriana*) and Korean fir (*Abies koreana*).

The historic Garden – When Sir John Naesmyth replaced Dawyck House, which had been destroyed by fire in 1830, he also added many built structures to the Garden. Many of the steps, balustrades and urns were added at this time, commissioned from a team of Italian landscape gardeners, with the iconic Dutch Bridge being added after 1856.

Follow our two themed tree trails, **Majestic Trees** and **Exotic Trees**, to see some of the most notable specimens in the Garden.

Native Scots Pine Wood – Seed collected in the 1850s in the forest of Mar in Aberdeenshire was carefully nurtured to establish Dawyck's own pocket of Caledonian pine forest. Now in majestic maturity it is a wonderful natural environment that can transport the imaginative visitor back in time to an original Caledon pine forest.

Sargent's Garden – Named after American Botanist Charles Sprague Sargent, this area celebrates the links between Dawyck, Harvard University's Arnold Arboretum (Sargent was the Arboretum's first Director) and the early distributions of seed collected by Ernest Wilson in China. Today Sargent's Garden is a tranquil burnside walk amongst unusual flowering herbaceous perennials.

Sargent's Garden

Ice Houses – Large houses with policy ground established these in caverns or underground chambers set into a north facing slopes and loaded up with ice and snow. Dawyck has two examples, so see if you can spot them both.

Dawyck House – The second generation house, built in 1832, was designed by William Burn. Grand in appearance, with an unusual collection of spires and turrets, the house is wider than it is deep, and thus appears larger than it is. It remains in private ownership.

Dawyck Chapel – The chapel is under the ownership of Dawyck Estate and is a very early example of a local place of worship. The existing building dates back to 1837 and houses a very early medieval font; the bell is said to date back to 1642. As a place of burial, the surrounding cemetery is the last resting place of many notable figures in the development of Dawyck.

Dutch Bridge – Dating back to the mid 1800s, the bridge was constructed to a Dutch design, which Sir John Naesmyth had enthused over on his travels abroad and arranged to have carefully replicated.

Sculptures

▼ **New Life** – Located just below the Dutch Bridge, on the eastern side of the Scrape Burn, blending perfectly with the many ferns that grow there (the shuttlecock fern, *Matteucia struthioperis*, and the sword fern, *Polystichum munitum*) is our sculpture 'New Life'. Hand crafted from Portland limestone by local sculptor Susheila Jamieson, it mirrors the unfurling fern fronds that surround it, peacefully promising a continuous cycle of regeneration. The piece was commissioned by Eric Ward, a longstanding supporter of the Garden and advocate of the woodland sanctuary. Eric grew up in the local area and on returning after many years decided to give something back to his childhood spiritual home.

Henderson Memorial Sculpture – This beautiful sculpture by Elizabeth Macdonald Buchanan was built in memory of Professor Douglas Mackay Henderson, the Regius Keeper who oversaw Dawyck's move into the care of RBGE. It celebrates Henderson's passion for the lower plant groups, now conserved and studied at the Heron Wood Reserve.

Native American Sculpture ▶ – Between the Dynamo Pond and Beech Walk you can find a chainsaw carving of a First Nations figure, representative of people of North America and British Columbia. Carved by Peter Bowsher from a tree felled at the Garden, it celebrates Dawyck's links with North America.

◀ **Gentle Presence** – Placed in the Garden in 2016, this sculpture was crafted from a one tonne piece of Portland limestone by artist Susheila Jamieson, to portray a sense of movement and calming energy. The delicate flowing lines suggest ideas of metamorphosis, evolution and transition, all naturally occurring processes reflected in the surrounding Garden setting.

Scrape Glen

Scrape Glen contains many notable trees, including those at the head of the Rhododendron Walk. A Grand fir (*Abies grandis*) and a Douglas fir (*Pseudotsuga menziesii*) sit boldly side by side like sentries watching over the Garden. Adjacent to Scrape Burn, the trees are early introductions of their type, with the Douglas fir cultivated from David Douglas' original seed, collected in the Pacific Northwest of America. In the spring and autumn the air here is filled with a characteristic caramel scent from the Japanese katsura tree (*Cercidiiphyllum japonicum*) that grows nearby. This part of the Garden is popular early in the season, with visitors appreciating the drifts of snowdrops that clothe the Glen from early February. Naturalised *Galanthus nivalis* and some snowflakes (*Leucojum vernum*) break the winter dormancy with their characteristic drops of milk-white amongst the greens and browns of the banks.

Galanthus nivalis

Picea breweriana

Larix decidua

Pseudotsuga menziesii

Heritage trees

Dawyck is home to some old and notable trees. Here is a selection to look out for.

Silver fir (*Abies alba*): Planted in 1680, this is the oldest tree in the Garden. Situated on the edge of Heron Wood, it is native to the mountains of Europe.

European larch (*Larix decidua*): This tree, which overlooks the Dynamo Pond, was reputedly planted at Dawyck in 1725 in the presence of Carl Linnaeus, the forefather of plant nomenclature and classification.

Douglas fir (*Pseudotsuga menziesii*): Dawyck is home to many trees grown from seed collected by David Douglas himself, notably this multi-stemmed specimen located west of the Visitor Centre and planted in 1835.

Giant Redwood (*Sequoiadendron giganteum*): There are many of these North American giants in the Garden. All stand well in excess of 50 metres high.

Dawyck beech (*Fagus sylvatica* 'Dawyck'): Allegedly discovered around 1850 in woodland to the north of Dawyck House, this has become a world-renowned tree and the original still stands in good health.

Brewer's weeping spruce (*Picea breweriana*): this was originally observed by F.R.S. Balfour in the Pacific Northwest of America, and he arranged to have a number of seedlings dug up and shipped back to Dawyck. Planted out in 1912, most of the originals still survive, making Dawyck home to arguably the finest collection of these graceful conifers in the world.

Sequoiadendron giganteum

Chapel Bank

This area of the Garden is a good place to appreciate some of the original rhododendron plantings for which Dawyck is well known, some of them in excess of 100 years old. *Rhododendron wardii* bears bright yellow-cupped flowers, while *Rhododendron alutaceum* has leathery, hair-covered leaves and a faint smell of cocoa. An unusual, mature castor oil tree (*Kalopanax septemlobus*) can be seen in this area. It is native to Japan and China, so is well suited to the climate at Dawyck, and has a very ornamental appearance. From the ivy family, Araliaceae, it has jagged leaves, shaped like huge hands, which turn a rich yellow in the autumn. Near the Dutch Bridge there is a mature Tibetan cherry (*Prunus serrula*), distinctive with its smooth red bark peeling in strips as a process of self-renewal. This tree looks wonderful in the winter with a blanket of snow all around, while in summer it bears white scented flowers. Autumn crocuses adorn this bank twice a year, producing leaves in the spring and flowers in the autumn.

Chapel Bank leading to the Dutch Bridge

Kalopanax septemlobus

Rhododendron wardii

Colchicum autumnale

A green Garden

Dawyck became the first carbon neutral botanic garden in the UK in 2014 when our hydroelectric scheme was launched. Back at the turn of the 20th century, Dawyck House was amongst pioneering private houses in Scotland installing their own hydroelectricity systems. Using the power of Scrape Burn – the Tweed tributary that runs through the Garden – we saw the opportunity to reinstate a similar, modern system at the Garden today as part of our responsible environmental management. This means that the Visitor Centre is almost entirely powered by electricity we generate ourselves, with any excess generation being fed back to the National Grid.

Changes in demand mean that we have to constantly keep up with new opportunities to ensure that the Garden remains green for years to come. The hydro turbine was improved in 2016/17 which has enhanced generation. As part of RBGE's new Carbon Management Plan, there will be further improvements to energy efficiency and renewable generation at Dawyck, with the upcoming installation of some new solar panels helping us on our way towards Net Zero.

All of the heating and hot water for staff and visitors at the Garden is provided by our wood-fuelled biomass boiler. We use locally-sourced woodchip, from soft-wood forestry thinning and plank manufacturing, with the minimal ash from the boiler added to our compost heap. Both the Visitor Centre and the hydro-electric turbine

house are insulated by green roofs, made up of low-growing, drought-tolerant sedum plants, as well as wild grasses and mosses. These special roofs keep us warm in winter and cool in summer, as well as providing a valuable habitat and food source for insects and other invertebrates.

The dynamo pond

The green garden in numbers

The Dawyck Hydroelectric turbine generates an average of 142 kWh a day or 51,947 kWh a year.

The average UK home uses 8kWh of electricity a day, which means that Dawyck produces enough to power 18 households at any given time.

Since installation, the hydro scheme has avoided 125 tonnes of carbon emissions, which is the equivalent of planting over 2,000 trees.

The turbine house

Metasequoia glyptostroboides

Endangered conifers

Of the world's 615 conifer species, 34 per cent are listed by the International Union for Conservation of Nature (IUCN) as being threatened. Based at RBGE, the International Conifer Conservation Programme (ICCP) was established in 1993 to help protect some of the world's most threatened conifer species. It is important to have specimens in cultivation as well as conserving plants in their wild habitats; in some cases preserving genetic resources in this way is the only option for critically endangered species. To do this we have established a network of 'safe sites' throughout the UK, and we currently have 145 sites where we have planted 13,000 trees.

Dawyck plays a hugely important role in this conservation initiative. It is home to a group of 12 trees collected from the Nebrodi Mountains in Sicily, the largest group of the critically endangered Sicilian fir (*Abies nebrodensis*) in cultivation. There are only 30 of these handsome trees left in their native habitat due to fires and historic logging. Look out for the Brewer's weeping spruce (*Picea breweriana*) in the Shaw Brae area of the Garden, this specimen was collected in 1908 by FRS Balfour of Dawyck House. With its long, pendulous branches draped in loose skirts of blue-green foliage, ours is one of the finest original collections of this unusual tree. In its natural habitat Brewer's spruce remains threatened, with only a few isolated groups growing in the Siskiyou Mountains in northwestern California. Recently, new conservation collections of this species have been strategically planted throughout the Garden to ensure its place at Dawyck for years to come. On either side of the Upper West Burn are 17 dawn redwood trees (*Metasequoia glyptostroboides*), grown from seed collected from isolated (and therefore especially threatened) trees in Metasequoia Valley in the Chinese Province of Hubei, where the tree is endangered. Other recently planted threatened species include the Serbian spruce (*Picea omorika*), the rarely cultivated Korean arbor-vitae (*Thuja koraiensis*) and several species from Chile including the plum yew (*Prumnopitys andina*) and the Alerce (*Fitzroya cupressoides*) near the western windbreak.

The cone of *Abies nebrodensis*

The bark of *Abies squamata*

A grove of *Abies nebrodensis*

Dawyck's Natural History

Despite being a created landscape with many non-native inhabitants, Dawyck is an ancient habitat with a wealth of wildlife and natural history. The diversity of the Garden - with varying woodland and open habitats, the burn, and slopes of differing aspects - means there is a large range of wildlife living here.

Lichens

Its dry summers and cool winters make Dawyck an important site in a network of RBGE experiments to understand the effects of climate change by studying lichens in Scotland. Research in this diverse landscape helps us to understand how the effects of global climate change might be modified by topography, such as the local effect of moisture from streams and rivers.

Bryophytes (mosses and liverworts)

There are an enormous number of bryophytes to be found at the Garden, with one rare moss species, *Orthotrichum pumilum*, which has been recorded at only four locations in Scotland.

Wildlife

Our last Bioblitz of the Garden, a 24-hour survey of wildlife species, resulted in a total count of 561 species at Dawyck. Here are some to look out for.

Brown trout – a healthy population resides in Scrape Burn

Herons – Heron Wood was the historic site of King James IV's heronry during his reign in the 15th century. Herons regularly nested at Dawyck until the 1968 hurricane destroyed the trees they used. They still visit the Garden though, and their presence is celebrated by the Heron Wood Reserve and in the Henderson memorial.

Red squirrels – a species now displaced by the grey squirrel (an introduction from America) over much of the UK. The Dawyck population is a rare survival away from Highland strongholds and is being monitored and conserved through local action.

Hares – not especially rare, but a nice larger mammal to look out for at the Garden, even if not always a welcome guest from a horticultural point of view.

Crossbills – a bird that has become adapted to eating conifer seeds and so is particularly associated with conifer forest.

Goldcrests – also have a particular liking for the habitat conifers provide.

Bumblebees – these large bees can be easily spotted in summer. Two species were recorded at the BioBlitz: *Bombus pascuorum* and *Bombus lucorum*.

Dawyck through the seasons

The Garden is known for its stunning azaleas and bright meconopsis blues in summer, but there is always colour and interest at Dawyck if you look for it. Up amongst the trees, or in the understorey plantings, shades of green and textures of cones and needles add richness to the foliage, while lichens, fungi and other lower plants provide surprises of colour and form throughout the seasons.

Spring

In early spring Dawyck is alive with snowdrops. The first flowers to push through the hard ground, they carpet the banks of Scrape Burn and climb the hillside behind. The butter-yellow flowers of winter aconites (*Eranthis hyemalis*) are a heartening sight through the gloom of winter, while a woodland walk is rewarded by the freshest of green beech leaves and the magnificent sight of the earliest flowering rhododendrons, including *Rhododendron strigilosum* and *Rhododendron oreodoxa.*

Rhododendron strigillosum

Abies firma

Summer

Summers here tend to be warmer and drier than the rest of Scotland. May and June are the best times to see the Azalea Terrace, with its colours burning bright against the greens of the Garden landscape. But late-flowering *Rhododendron maximum* and the azalea *Rhododendron occidentale* are often putting on a show into July. The cotoneasters are sprinkled liberally with their miniature flowers through June, while the meconopsis, one of the Himalayan natives that thrive in Dawyck's conditions, are best seen earlier in the season. Late summer is a good time to look beside Scrape Burn for astilbes enjoying the moist soil and shadier conditions beside lush hostas and ferns.

Rhododendron occidentale

Prunus Serrula

Autumn

Autumn is a glorious time at Dawyck. Seasonal colour is abundant, with reds, golds and rich browns from the maples, rowans, beech, spindle trees, the beautiful Japanese katsura candyfloss tree (*Cercidiphyllum japonicum*) and North American golden birch (*Betula alleghaniensis*). At your feet are autumn crocuses, spectacular fungi and fruits galore, prickly beech nut husks, fir cones, maple keys and shiny conkers.

Winter

The Garden slips into dormancy, and with the leaves off the trees it is an amazing time to marvel at their architecture, with the shapes and forms of the conifers and broadleaves more obvious without the main canopy. Winter frosts show off the striking colours of the bark, a contrast all the more dramatic when there is snow on the ground.

Managing the collection

There are five full-time Garden staff based at Dawyck, supported by nine volunteers. This small, but extremely versatile team deals with all aspects of maintenance from planting and weed control to hard landscaping and all types of arboriculture required in order to maintain Dawyck's status as a world-class woodland Garden.

Maintenance of a Garden like Dawyck presents all sorts of challenges. The exposure of the Garden to the westerly winds is never more evident than in winter when there are often casualties in the ageing tree population. It is very important to react positively to losses and look upon them as an opportunity for future replanting.

Dawyck in numbers

26 hectares

5 horticultural staff

9 volunteers

2 tractors

8 chainsaws

1,200mm average rainfall per year

80 plant families from 155 countries via 296 plant collectors

3,115 plant species of known wild origin

210 genera

38,000 visitors every year

SP14
BWY
AEBI

Reprinted 2022

ISBN: 978-1-910877-18-0

Images by: Mike Allport, Peter Clarke, Amy Copeman,
Alison Harris, Gavin Harris, David Hull, Eugene McCarron, John Roberts, Graham Stewart,
Stephen Talas, Bob Thomson, Mikuni Uehara, Robert Unwin, Lynsey Wilson

Text by Alice Young and Graham Stewart,
with thanks to Max Coleman, Chris Ellis and Martin Gardner

Design and layout by Caroline Muir

The Royal Botanic Garden Edinburgh is a Non Departmental Public Body (NDPB) sponsored and supported
through Grant-in-Aid by the Scottish Government's Environment and Forestry Directorate (ENFOR).
The Royal Botanic Garden Edinburgh is a Charity registered in Scotland (number SC007983).

All information correct at time of going to press.

Printed by McAllister Litho Glasgow Limited